Riches of the Earth

Pearls

Irene Franck and David Brownstone

GROLIER

An imprint of Scholastic Library Publishing
Danbury, Connecticut

Credits and Acknowledgments

abbreviations: t (top), b (bottom), l (left), r (right), c (center)

Image credits: Karen Alexander, Big River Buttons: 8r; Art Resource: 6 and 14 (Réunion des Musées Nationaux); 9, 11, and 13 (Scala); 12 (Erich Lessing); CORBIS: 16 (Reuters Newsmedia, Inc.); Getty Images: 4 (Stone/BZB), 5 (Stone/Martin Barraud), 17 (Image Bank/Derek Berwin), 20 (PhotoDisc/Ian Cartwright), 21r (PhotoDisc/C Squared Studios); Library of Congress: 18; National Aeronautics and Space Administration (NASA): 1t and running heads; National Geographic Society: 7 (Jodi Cobb), 19 (Gilbert M. Grosvenor), 21l (Bruce Dale); Photo Researchers, Inc.: 1 and 29r (Vaughan Fleming/Science Photo Library), 8l (Thomas R. Taylor), 10 (Sylvain Grandadam), 22 (Philippe Roy/Explorer), 25 (Robert A. Isaacs), 26 (Bill Bachman), 29l (Frederick Ayer); U.S. Department of Defense: 28 (Lt. Chuck Radosta, U.S. Navy); Woodfin Camp & Associates: 3 (Walter Hodges); 23l, 23r, and 27 (Ettagale Blauer); 24 (Mike Yamashita). Original image drawn for this book by K & P Publishing Services: 15.

Our thanks to Joe Hollander, Phil Friedman, and Laurie McCurley at Scholastic Library Publishing; to photo researchers Susan Hormuth, Robin Sand, and Robert Melcak; to copy editor Michael Burke; and to the librarians throughout the northeastern library network, in particular to the staff of the Chappaqua Library—director Mark Hasskarl; the expert reference staff, including Martha Alcott, Michele J. Capozzella, Maryanne Eaton, Catherine Paulsen, Jane Peyraud, Paula Peyraud, and Carolyn Reznick; and the circulation staff, headed by Barbara Le Sauvage—for fulfilling our wide-ranging research needs.

Published 2003 by Grolier
Division of Scholastic Library Publishing
Old Sherman Turnpike
Danbury, Connecticut 06816

For information address the publisher:
Scholastic Library Publishing, Grolier Division
Old Sherman Turnpike, Danbury, Connecticut 06816

© 2003 Irene M. Franck and David M. Brownstone

All rights reserved. Except for use in a review, no part of this book may be reproduced, stored in a retrieval system, or transmitted in any form, or by any means, electronic or mechanical, including photocopying, recording, or otherwise, without prior permission of Scholastic Library Publishing.

Library of Congress Cataloging-in-Publication Data

Franck, Irene M.
    Pearls / Irene Franck and David Brownstone.
      p. cm. -- (Riches of the earth ; v. 7)
    Summary: Provides information about pearls and their importance in everyday life.
    Includes bibliographical references and index.
    ISBN 0-7172-5730-4 (set : alk. paper) -- ISBN 0-7172-5719-3 (vol. 7 : alk paper)
    1. Pearls--Juvenile literature [1. Pearls.] I. Brownstone, David M. II. Title.

NK7680.F73 2003
639'.412--dc21

2003044083

Printed in the United States of America

Designed by K & P Publishing Services

Contents

Beautiful Pearls 4

What Are Pearls? 6

Pearls in History 11

Pearl Diving 17

Pearl Farming 22

Dangers for Pearls 26

Words to Know 30

On the Internet 31

In Print 31

Index 32

Beautiful Pearls

Pearls come in many colors, ranging from creamy white to black. They also take on the color of their surroundings, reflecting back colors around them, as this pearl does with its blue background.

The most beautiful of the gemstones called pearls seem to glow, to shine with deep, brilliant, inner radiance. At the same time they catch and play an ever-changing rainbow of light across their surfaces. That deep radiant glow is *luster*, and the rainbow display of light is *iridescence*, in pearls often called *orient*. Of all the qualities of pearls, luster and orient are by far the most highly prized, in many cultures and for thousands of years.

All true pearls are hard growths within the living bodies of soft-bodied shellfish called *mollusks*. Mollusks, in turn, are part of the much larger group of animals called *invertebrates*, because they have no backbones or spinal columns. (*Vertebrates*, such as humans and cats, do have backbones.)

Our planet holds tens of thousands of kinds of mollusks, most of whom live in the salt seas or freshwater lakes and rivers. Many of

Beautiful Pearls

these kinds of mollusks grow pearls in their bodies—yet only very few grow pearls of gemstone quality. The huge numbers of mollusks that we eat for food, including many kinds of oysters and mussels, very rarely produce high-quality pearls.

The kinds of mollusks that produce gemstone-quality pearls are often called "pearl oysters." However, that is only a general description, rather than a name for specific kinds of oysters. These pearl-producing mollusks are mainly hardshelled *bivalve* oysters and mussels. That means they have a shell with two halves joined by a hinge. For thousands of years the highest quality saltwater pearls have been found in just a few kinds of pearl oysters, and the highest quality freshwater pearls in a few kinds of mussels (see p. 6).

Saltwater and freshwater pearls found in their natural settings are *natural pearls*. However, many pearls today are cultivated (grown) by pearl farmers; these are called *cultured pearls*. Whether natural or cultured, all are true pearls, though with some differences (see p. 9). Large numbers of imitation pearls are also made. These look like pearls, but are not real pearls at all.

Oysters and mussels are *bivalves*—that is, they have shells that open in two halves, joined by a hinge. This is the open shell of an oyster with a pearl inside (though the living body of the oyster itself is gone).

Large, well-shaped pearls were reserved for special purposes and especially rich people. These perfectly matched enormous pear-shaped pearl earrings belonged to France's Empress Josephine, wife of Emperor Napoleon Bonaparte.

What Are Pearls?

Pearls are the result of a natural process that starts when a small bit of foreign matter finds its way into the shell (*mantle*) of a mollusk (see p. 4). This foreign matter comes to rest inside the living mollusk's soft body, either between the mantle and the mantle's lining, or else inside the lining itself. In the few kinds of mollusks that grow high-quality pearls, that lining is made of *mother-of-pearl* (*nacre*), from which pearls will grow.

In what become natural pearls, the bit of foreign matter that gets inside the mollusk may be a tiny worm that cuts its way into the mantle, another very small creature, or a bit of any other kind of material. Very rarely, it may even be a grain of sand.

Not all saltwater oysters and freshwater mussels form gemstone pearls. In those that do so, the bit of matter inside the mantle becomes the *nucleus* (center) of a pearl. Seeking to protect its soft inner body from the hard foreign object from outside, the mollusk wraps around the nucleus many thin layers

What Are Pearls?

of mother-of-pearl, drawn from its lining.

Many pearls go no further than the space between the mantle and its mother-of-pearl lining. To protect itself, the mollusk draws on its mother-of-pearl lining to grow a smooth, hard wall that covers the rough foreign object and holds it between the mantle and the lining. The pearls so formed are called *blister pearls*, because they form only small bulges on the inner lining of the shell.

Other pearls form themselves around muscle tissue inside the body of the mollusk. Sometimes quite large and irregularly shaped, these are called *baroque pearls*. Some of the largest baroque pearls have become extremely valuable, very highly regarded pieces of jewelry.

Most gemstone-quality natural pearls grow freely inside the body of the mollusk. There they can reach their natural size and shape, losing none of their luster, orient, and overall beauty. These are natural

When foreign objects get in between the oyster's mantle (shell) and its lining, the oyster grows a layer over them to protect itself. The result is blister pearls, like those in this open oyster.

Pearls

pearls, also called *free pearls*. These form when hard, small foreign objects get past the inner wall of the mantle. Then the mollusk grows many thin layers of pearl drawn from the inner lining of the mantle all the way around the foreign object. This forms a *pearl sac*, which in turn becomes the pearl itself.

Pearls formed out of such pearl sacs tend to be round and many-layered. They look much like onions, though made of very different materials. However, very few pearls are completely smooth and round. Whether natural or cultured, most pearls have somewhat rough and uneven surfaces.

The sizes and weights of gemstone-quality pearls vary a great deal, depending mainly on the sizes and kinds of mollusks in which they grow. On the low end large quantities of pearls are so tiny and light

(Right) Mollusk shells lined with mother-of-pearl have long been valued for themselves, not just for pearl-making. These are mother-of-pearl buttons, plus a shell from which two buttons have been cut, taken from the Mississippi River.

(Below) Pearls are formed from the mollusk lining called, very aptly, *mother-of-pearl* (*nacre*). The lining itself also has both luster and color highlights (*orient*), as shown here.

What Are Pearls?

Today smooth, round pearls are most desired. However, during much of history misshapen pearls, called *baroque pearls*, were also highly prized, since they could be used to make striking jewelry, like these pendants from Italy, with the baroque pearls forming the bodies of a seahorse (left) and a hare.

that they are called *dust pearls*, and great masses of larger but still small pearls are called *seed pearls*. On the very high end, a huge natural pearl named the Pearl of Allah weighs more than 12.7 pounds!

The basic difference between natural and cultured pearls is this: In cultured pearls the hard, small foreign object that forms the nucleus of the pearl is deliberately inserted into the mollusk shell, rather than finding its own way in by natural means (see p. 22).

Content of Pearls

All true pearls, whether natural or cultured, are made of the same materials. The main material in almost all pearls, making up about 85 percent to 90 percent of the pearl, is *aragonite*. This is a crystal form of the chemical compound (mixed substance) *calcium carbonate*, made of the elements (basic substances) *calcium* and *carbon*. Most of the rest of the pearl is made of *conchiolin*, a thin layer of tissue created within the body of the mollusk. The rest of the pearl is made of water and small traces of other elements. Within the pearl the conchiolin is mixed with the thin sheets of aragonite that make up most of the pearl.

Though strong enough to resist direct smashing, pearls are easily

Pearls

attacked by many acids. They also crack easily, as when they are being drilled for stringing on a necklace or when they become too dry.

Some "pearls" are not pearls at all. These are the synthetic or imitation pearls, which are made in very large quantities throughout the world. Synthetic pearls have been created for thousands of years as very good-looking costume jewelry but sometimes as a fake substitute for the real thing.

Color

Natural pearls have a wide range of colors, all the way from pure white to deep black, including all the other colors of the rainbow in between. All of these colors stem from the colors inside the shells of the mollusks that produce them.

In cultured pearls the range of colors is also very wide. There the colors come from the beads of pearl and other materials from which the cultured pearls grow.

Pearls come in many different colors, shapes, and sizes. These earrings from the South Pacific island of Tahiti are called "black pearls," though they are really a deep and beautiful shade of blue.

All around the world the rich and royal draped themselves in pearls. The sixth-century A.D. Byzantine Roman empress Theodora is shown here with pearls decorating her headdress and gown. The pearls are represented by small white circles and teardrop shapes in this mosaic, a work of art made of small pieces of stone.

Pearls in History

Pearls have played a role in history for thousands of years. Archaeologists have found pearl jewelry and pearls used as religious objects at sites 3,000 to 4,000 years old throughout the Middle East. By 2,500 years ago pearls were highly valued in many of the civilizations of the ancient world. In the Roman Empire, for example, high-quality pearls became jewels of enormous value. Large, greatly valuable pearls were worn only by Roman royalty and other very wealthy Romans. However, less expensive pearl jewelry was also in great demand.

Pearls were also gemstones of great value in India. Indian rulers

Pearls

and their treasuries gathered huge stores of all kinds of gems, including pearls. Indian Hindu and Buddhist temples also had much-valued stores of pearls and other gems.

In India pearls were also used in medicine. Usually crushed into powders, they were dissolved in such liquids as lemon juice or used in salves (medicinal ointments). Pearls were believed to cure a very wide range of illnesses, all the way from blood and heart diseases to eyesight and dental problems.

Pearls were also highly prized in the Muslim world, which expanded into a great empire more than a thousand years ago. As in India, which was the source of much of Muslim medical knowledge, pearls were thought to cure many illnesses.

Chinese medicine also used pearls in powders, liquids, and salves to treat many illnesses. Chinese doctors prescribed pearl medicines to bring long life, to act against poisons, and for many other purposes.

Ancient Pearl Fisheries

The three greatest pearl fishing grounds of the ancient world were all in the western part of the Indian Ocean. They were all so connected that they are often seen as a single

For much of history pearls were the equals of gold, silver, diamonds, and other precious gems, as in this crown. It was made in what is now Germany in about 962 A.D. for Otto I, emperor of the Holy Roman Empire.

Pearls in History

The 1500s, when pearls started arriving in Europe in large numbers, is sometimes called the "Great Age of Pearls." This portrait of England's Queen Elizabeth I shows her wearing not only long ropes of pearls and a pearl necklace but also pearls as decorations in her hair and on the fan-like structure behind her shoulders, as well as pearls sewn all over her fancy collar and gown.

pearling (pearl fishing) area, producing most of the high-quality saltwater pearls of the ancient world.

The largest, oldest, and most productive of these pearling grounds was the Persian Gulf, today far better known for its oil than for its pearls. One of the major pearl fisheries of the Gulf was located in what is now Bahrain (earlier Dilmun). Other major fisheries in the Gulf were in what are now Oman, the United Arab Emirates, Saudi Arabia, Qatar, Kuwait, Iraq, and Iran.

Pearls

Pearls and other precious stones were highly valued in the ancient world and on into modern times. This pendant, shaped like a bird, was made in India in the 1600s of pearls, diamonds, rubies, emeralds, gold, and rock crystal.

The second of the three major ancient fisheries was in the Red Sea, between Saudi Arabia and East Africa. The third was in the Gulf of Mannar, between Sri Lanka (formerly Ceylon) and the southern tip of India.

Substantial saltwater pearl fisheries were also found in other parts of the ancient world, most notably in Southeast Asia. High-quality saltwater pearl fisheries existed off the southern Chinese coast as long as 2,000 years ago. These were in what are now the Chinese provinces of Guangxi and Guangzhou, the island of Hainan, and northern Vietnam (then Annam), which was for many centuries part of China.

Starting as early as 2,500 years ago, large quantities of freshwater pearls were also taken from many rivers and lakes throughout China and other regions of East Asia, including what are now Mongolia and Siberia. Freshwater pearls were also fished throughout Central Asia.

Pearls in the New World

Great saltwater pearl fisheries were also found in Central America, the Caribbean, and northern South America. Major freshwater pearl mussel fisheries existed in the huge Mississippi River system, in what would later become the United States. These fisheries supplied large numbers of pearls to the peoples of the Americas.

High-quality pearls became prized jewelry in some American cultures. Pearls also became religious objects for some American peoples, among

Pearls in History

them the Mayans, Toltecs, and Aztecs. However, American pearls were not known to the rest of the world until the Columbus voyages of the 1490s.

Long before the Columbus voyages to the New World, pearls were being gathered in the pearl fisheries of the Caribbean and Central America. The greatest of all American pearl fishing grounds were those off the Caribbean coast of Venezuela. The Spanish would later call that stretch of coastline the Pearl Coast and America would be named the Land of Pearls.

During Columbus's first two voyages to the Americas (1492 and 1493), he failed to find major sources of pearls. In his third voyage (1498), however, he found Venezuela's Pearl Coast. With that began a major period of Spanish pearl-gathering. In just half a century more than a billion oysters were harvested, which yielded hundreds of thousands of pearls. Beyond Venezuela, huge masses of pearls were also gathered in Panama, Mexico, Nicaragua, and from many other locations.

The Spanish pearl harvest of that time was so huge that it flooded Europe with pearls. For European rulers, nobles, and moneyed people

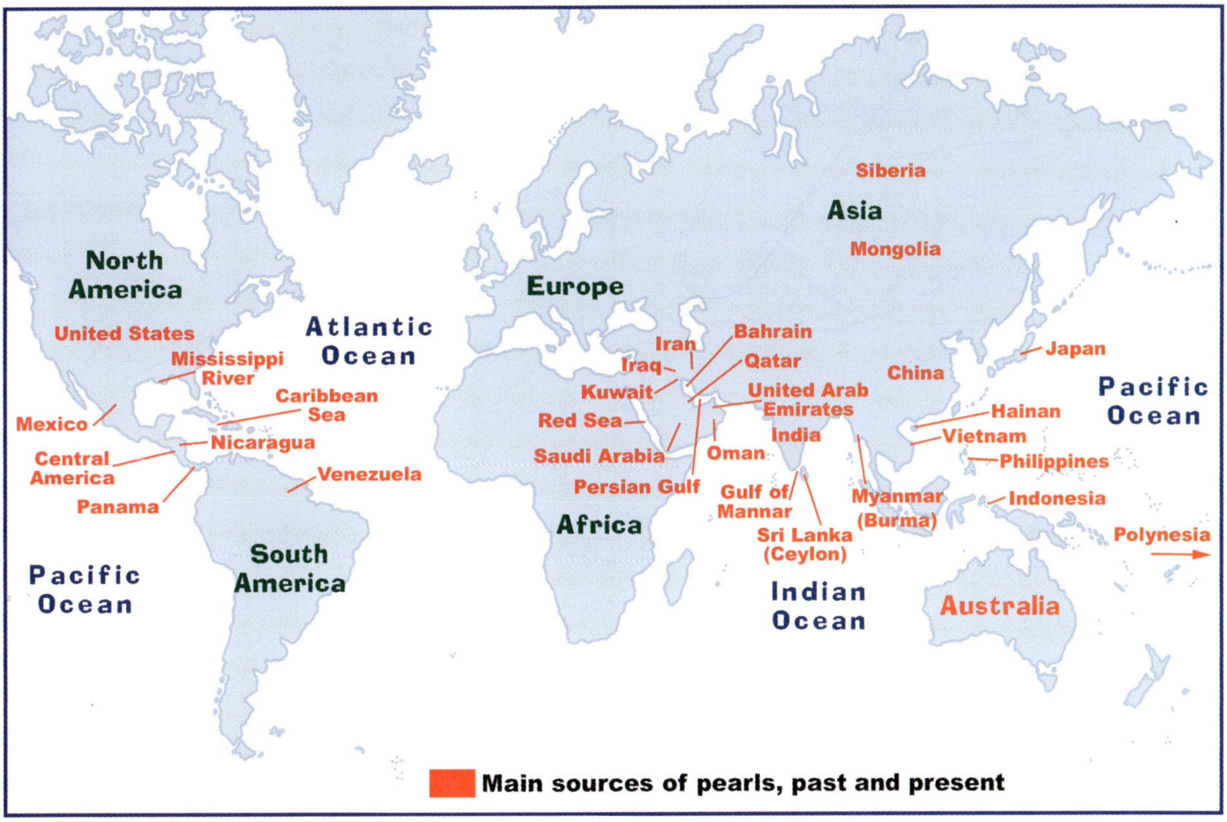

Main sources of pearls, past and present

Pearls

of all kinds, the collection and display of large quantities of valuable pearls became a "must." Women of enormous wealth, among them queens and princesses, displayed pearls in many forms, worn as necklaces, headdresses, belts, and earrings, and also sewn into articles of clothing. Pearls became so popular—and profitable—that even Spanish efforts to control the pearl trade failed.

By the 1550s, only half a century after the huge trade in American pearls began, few high-quality pearls were still there to be fished on Venezuela's Pearl Coast. Pearls, however, continued to be tremendously popular as gemstones. Saltwater natural pearls were still gathered in many other parts of the world, including the great Indian Ocean fisheries.

Freshwater pearls kept their popularity, as well. They continued to be widely used in jewelry and sewn in large quantities into clothing.

Though pearls are available to many people now, they continue to be favored by the rich and royal. This is Britain's late Princess Diana, wearing a tiara featuring large droplet pearls along with large pearl earrings. Her dress is also studded with small seed pearls.

This woman is free-diving underwater, without any breathing aids. However, in real life she would never find a pearl as big as this one—which is clearly too big to fit in the shell!

Pearl-carrying saltwater oysters are found on the sea floor. Pearl-carrying freshwater mussels are found on the floors of lakes and streams.

In very early times, in places that had been little fished, people could just walk out into shallow water and scoop up oysters, take them ashore, and open them up, looking for pearls. However, that did not last long, for the oysters near the shore were soon used up. Then it was necessary to fish for pearl oysters by diving for them. Diving has been the main way of pearl fishing for thousands of years, probably starting at least 5,000 years ago in the Persian Gulf and the Red Sea. Freshwater mussels also became harder to fish and required diving.

For thousands of years the basic process of diving for pearls varied very little from region to region throughout the world. The pearl-diving process also changed little over time, until the early 1800s, with the invention of diving suits and helmets that allowed divers to breathe underwater.

First divers had to reach the oys-

Pearls

ter beds by boat. The kinds of boats used did vary widely, from a small one-person dugout canoe (in later times, perhaps a fast motorboat) to a large commercial vessel. Some large Gulf of Mannar or Persian Gulf ships might carry a crew of 60, among them 25 pearl divers.

Pearl diving itself was hardly ever the kind of showy diving you might see in an old movie. Divers did not make a high dive into the water, but instead a far less exhausting short and easy dive from the boat. Holding their breath, divers would enter the water either feet-first or head-first, depending on the standard method used in the region. Each normally carried a weight of 30 or more pounds, to make it possible to stay down on the ocean floor.

The depth of the dive would depend on the depth of the ocean floor. The deeper the dive, the riskier it was for the diver. The normal dive would range from roughly 35 feet to 70 feet (about 10 to 20 meters), though some divers would go much deeper, even as deep as 150 feet (about 45 meters) or even more.

Once on the bottom, the diver would gather several shells (often 5 to 15) in a basket, let go of the

Traditional pearl divers worked without any breathing aids. Then in the early 1800s diving suits and helmets were developed to supply them with air underwater. The suits were very cumbersome (and expensive), though, so many divers continued to work unaided. This drawing of a diver in suit and helmet dates from 1915.

In some parts of the world workers continue to dive for pearls with no aid or protection. The best known of them are Japan's women divers, like this one shown diving with only a pair of goggles and a basket to fill.

weight, and return to the surface. The weight would be hauled up to the boat by rope, for use on the next dive. Through all this—from hitting the water to reaching the air on the way back up—divers would hold their breath. Most pearl divers wore nose clips to prevent their breathing in water.

Dangers for Divers

Pearl diving was a terribly dangerous occupation. Many divers suffered hearing loss or were seriously injured because of the effects of water pressure, a main problem for divers.

The pressure of air or water on an unprotected human body increases greatly as divers move deeper down in the water. The weight of air pressure on a body at sea level is called one *atmosphere*. The same body, 33 feet deep in water, has twice the pressure on it, described as "two atmospheres." At deeper water levels much higher pressures occur.

At high pressures the gas nitro-

Pearls

gen, always present in our bodies, moves into the body's blood and tissues. If the diver rises slowly in the water, the nitrogen disappears harmlessly. However, if the diver rises too quickly, nitrogen can cause very painful, damaging, and sometimes life-threatening nitrogen gas bubbles in the blood. This condition is called *decompression sickness* or more popularly "the bends."

Many modern divers wear special scuba gear, offering air tanks carried on the divers' backs, so they can breathe underwater. (*Scuba* is short for "self-contained underwater breathing apparatus.") This allows them to rise slowly. If they must rise quickly, they can go into special decompression chambers, which change the pressure gradually and safely.

A related major problem was that divers going down to the bottom too fast experienced a quick buildup of water pressure on their eardrums. Divers' ears were partially protected by being sealed with cotton or other substances. Even so, all too often their eardrums broke under the pressure, causing damage and deafness.

With modern scuba gear divers carry tanks of air on their backs, so they can stay underwater for a long time. This diver in scuba gear and wet suit is exploring the sea life underwater in the Indian Ocean, home of the greatest natural pearl fisheries.

Pearl Diving

These are shells from just a few of the tens of thousands of different kinds of oysters and mussels. Only a few kinds produce pearls of gem quality.

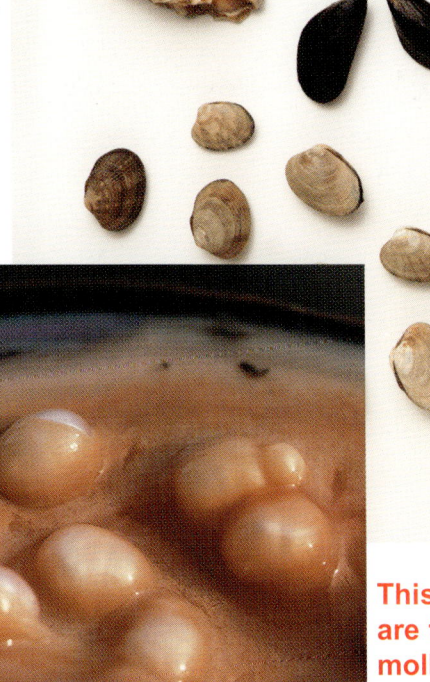

This is what pearls look like as they are forming in the shell of a living mollusk. Divers may have to open many oysters or mussels to find one that contains natural pearls.

Throughout history pearl divers have often been slaves or very poor people who could be forced to do whatever their employers required. As a result the divers very often had to work too fast and with too little protection, causing the bends, deafness, and other major injuries. Few laws protecting pearl divers were adopted anywhere in the world—and very few of such laws were ever enforced. The net effect was that pearl diving was for thousands of years an extremely dangerous occupation.

Diving for natural pearls can still be dangerous. However, it has become much less so today, with the use of scuba gear.

Beyond that, the whole world of pearls has changed a great deal since the introduction of cultured pearls in the early 1900s. Today most pearls are cultured pearls, cultivated by pearl farmers in many countries (see p. 22).

21

This woman is working in a pearl farm off the coast of France. She is holding one basket of oysters, with some other baskets already underwater and sitting on the jetty.

Pearl Farming

Pearl farming, called *perliculture*, is the creation of cultured (meaning cultivated) pearls on a water farm. That kind of water farming is also often called *aquaculture*, because *aqua* is the Latin word for "water."

Many divers still go after natural pearls. However, throughout the world the farming of cultured saltwater pearls has now largely replaced diving for natural saltwater pearls. That is a recent development, going back only to the early 1900s.

Freshwater pearls have been farmed in China for more than 2,000 years. Early Chinese pearl farmers opened the shells of living pearl mussels, inserted small foreign objects between the outer and inner

Pearl Farming

shells of the mussels, closed the mussel shells again, and returned the mussels to the water. The mussels stayed in the water for a year or more, while mother-of-pearl (nacre) grew inside the mussel shell, forming a blister pearl (see p. 7). Then the mussel was opened again, and the newly formed blister pearl was harvested.

Another farming technique was later developed in China and spread to Europe. It involved drilling a small hole and inserting a small foreign object in the pearl mussel shell, returning the mussel shell to water, and later harvesting the pearls cultivated in this way. Into the late 1800s Europeans experimented with this technique, which then spread back to the Far East. There it was used and developed further in several countries.

Japanese pearl farmer Kochiki

Small round pieces from the shell of the pigtoe clam (like those in the boxes above) are inserted into the shells of pearl-making oysters. Each one serves as the nucleus for a new pearl. This worker (at left) in the Japanese cultured pearl industry opens the oyster's shell and inserts one or more nuclei. The oyster's shell is then closed again and it is returned to the water where, if all goes well, it will grow cultured pearls.

Pearls

Mikimoto did not invent modern pearl cultivation. However, he was the first to turn pearl farming into a successful business. His pearl-farming methods, introduced in the early 1900s, were widely adopted by Japanese pearl farmers and later by pearl farmers throughout the world. Although now developed even further, they are still the basis of today's pearl-farming techniques.

The basic process of pearl farming starts with finding a healthy living oyster or mussel that is large enough to take the kind of pearl the farmer is trying to cultivate. This can be done by raising the right kinds of oysters and mussels. Divers can also find them growing wild. If diving, however, they use scuba gear (see p. 19), rather than diving in the old, terribly dangerous way.

If oysters or mussels are being raised on a pearl farm, they must first go through as much as two years of growth and preparation. If they are mature mollusks taken in the wild, they are ready much sooner.

The most important part of the process comes next. That is the implantation (insertion) of the bit of matter that will become the oyster's

Working in the modern cultured pearl industry, this woman is collecting oysters off Meixhou Island in the South China Sea.

nucleus, along with the white bead of inner mussel shell from which the new pearl's nacre will grow. This process is called *grafting*, *seeding*, or *nucleation*.

The nucleus is usually a round white bead taken from the shell of a Mississippi Valley mussel. This has been cut to produce the largest possible round white pearl practical for the size of the oyster being used. The nacre-producing material is taken from the inner shell of an oyster or mussel of the kind wanted by the pearl farmer. From this material layers of nacre will grow around the nucleus of the new pearl. In a single oyster one or two grafts are usually made in the open body of the live oyster or mussel.

After grafting, new pearls begin to grow in the oysters. While they are growing, the pearl farmer moves the oysters twice. First they are moved to carefully watched containers attached to rafts near the grafting area. Later they are moved a little farther away. Then the oysters are held in subsurface baskets attached to rafts for as much as two to three years (though usually less), while nacre grows around the new pearls that have been created. The developing oysters and their pearls are closely watched and cared for during this period of cultivation.

Working in Japan's cultured pearl industry, in the company founded by Kochiki Mikimoto, this woman is sorting pearls and matching them by size to prepare them for stringing, like the strands of already-strung pearls in the foreground.

Waste from human activities, including household detergents and farm fertilizers, can create an explosion in the numbers of tiny beings in the water, such as this "red tide" off Australia's northwest coast. It produces a poison that can kill oysters and mussels.

Dangers for Pearls

Beautiful pearls grow within the living bodies of healthy mollusks. However, many kinds of mollusks are very fragile creatures, right on the edge of survival. That is because they live on sea floors, along seacoasts and riverbanks, and in estuaries where rivers and seas meet— all places that have become very dangerous for them.

One such place is Chesapeake Bay, which Native Americans called the "Great Shellfish Bay." Located off the Maryland and Virginia coastline, the 180-mile-long bay has long been one of the world's great fish-

Dangers for Pearls

ing grounds. It is famed for its crabs and oysters, the best known of its more than 200 kinds of fish and shellfish, along with its thousands of other kinds of plants and animals.

The great bay has in modern times become polluted with ever-increasing masses of industrial and human waste from the farms, towns, and cities along the rivers that flow into the bay. Beyond that, huge quantities of such nutrients as household detergents and farm fertilizers have been dumped into these waters. These have triggered population growth in massive numbers of tiny plants, which foul the bay's water and also cause other kinds of pollution that threaten fish, plants, and people. Major attempts to clean up the bay have had some success, but growing populations and toxic waste dumping continue to add to the pollution.

The kind of hazardous situation threatening Chesapeake Bay is duplicated throughout the world. Unfortunately, most oysters and other shellfish live—and normally thrive—in just such now-threatened places.

Farmed mollusks are no better protected than those still growing "wild." The gemstone oysters so successfully developed in Japan, for example, are very seriously threatened by all the same factors that threaten the oysters of Chesapeake Bay. In earlier times pearl farmers

To help fight disease and pollution that can affect oysters, workers at this Japanese cultured pearl farm clean the oysters about twice a month.

Pearls

The Persian Gulf has historically been the home of the world's finest pearl fisheries, but the sea and the beings living in it have been damaged by spills from oil rigs like this one topped by a gas flare. Some of the spills have been triggered by frequent wars in the region.

normally allowed three years for nacre to grow after grafting. However, now six months to two years is more common, as pearl farmers try to limit damaging the oysters' exposure to pollution and disease.

Beyond these kinds of growing worldwide dangers, specific events can also pose immense dangers. Perhaps the best known of these was the tremendous damage done to the great Persian Gulf fishing grounds in the 1980s and 1990s by the oil spills and oil well fires of the Iran-Iraq War and the Gulf War. Many major oil spills, as from offshore drilling disasters or damaged oil tankers, have also caused great damage to pearl oysters, along with many other plants and animals. One of these was the blowout of the Ixtoc I well in Campeche Bay in the Gulf of Mexico, which in 1979 spilled 600,000 tons of crude oil into the bay.

The same dangers that affect saltwater pearl oysters and other saltwater fish also affect freshwater

Dangers for Pearls

pearl mussels. For example, the pigtoe mussel has long been the main North American source of the beads used in pearl farm grafting. However, it has for some years been a threatened species. Pearl farmers have had to switch to other freshwater mussels for their main sources of the vital beads.

Yet with all the growing dangers, large quantities of gemstone-quality natural pearls are still found around the world, and far larger and increasing amounts of cultured pearls are being farmed. Many nations have programs aimed at developing cultured pearl industries. Some of the most successful of these have been developed in Australia, China, Polynesia, Mexico, the Philippines, Indonesia, Myanmar (Burma), and several other Southeast Asian countries.

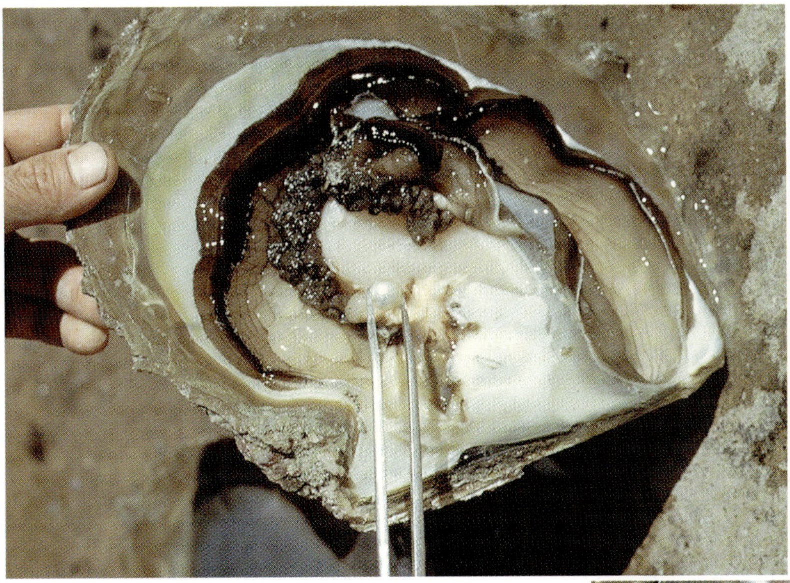

(Above) This pearl, being removed from an oyster with tweezers, could only have been grown by a living mollusk. Many oysters and mussels are now threatened by disease and pollution, mostly triggered by human activities. That includes the freshwater mollusks that produced these pearls (at right).

Words to Know

aquaculture: See PERLICULTURE.
aragonite The crystal form of *calcium carbonate*, a substance composed of the elements (basic substances) calcium and carbon. Aragonite makes up 85 percent to 90 percent of a pearl.
baroque pearl An irregularly shaped pearl that forms around muscle tissue inside the body of a MOLLUSK.
bends A painful and dangerous condition caused by the formation of nitrogen bubbles in a diver's blood and body tissues; also called *decompression sickness*. The bubbles go away normally if a diver rises back to the surface slowly but can be damaging and even life-threatening if the diver rises too quickly.
bivalve A kind of MOLLUSK with two halves joined by a hinge, including oysters and mussels that form pearls.
blister pearls Pearls that form between the *mantle* (outer shell) and the inner lining of a MOLLUSK.
calcium carbonate: See ARAGONITE.
conchiolin A thin layer of tissue that is created within the body of a MOLLUSK. It makes up 5 percent to 10 percent of a pearl.
cultured pearls Pearls cultivated by pearl farmers. They are formed by GRAFTING an oyster NUCLEUS and a mussel shell bead into a living oyster or mussel.
decompression sickness: See BENDS.
dust pearls Pearls that are so light and tiny that they look like dust.
free pearls: See NATURAL PEARLS.
freshwater pearls Pearls grown in the bodies of MOLLUSKS that live in freshwater bodies, such as lakes, rivers, and streams.
grafting Implanting inside an oyster a bit of foreign matter that will be the NUCLEUS of a pearl, along with a bead of inner mussel shell from which a new pearl will grow. Also called *seeding* or *nucleation*.
imitation pearls Small, round objects that are made to look like true pearls but are actually made of other substances; also called *synthetic pearls*. Generally used in inexpensive costume jewelry.
implantation: See GRAFTING.
invertebrate A large group of animals, including MOLLUSKS, that have no backbone or spinal column.

iridescence: See ORIENT.
luster The quality of a pearl that makes it glow with a deep, brilliant inner radiance.
mantle: See BLISTER PEARLS.
mollusk A soft-bodied INVERTEBRATE shellfish. Among the tens of thousands of varieties of mollusks are many kinds of oysters and mussels, but only a few grow gemstone-quality pearls.
mother-of-pearl: See NACRE.
nacre The inner shell of certain MOLLUSKS, such as PEARL OYSTERS, from which pearls grow; also called *mother-of-pearl*.
natural pearls Pearls that grow freely inside the body of a MOLLUSK; also called *free pearls*.
nucleation: See GRAFTING.
nucleus A bit of foreign matter that gets inside the body of a MOLLUSK, around which a pearl may grow. In CULTURED PEARLS the nucleus is deliberately placed inside the mollusk in a process called GRAFTING.
orient The quality that makes a pearl's surface shine with a constantly changing rainbow display of light; also called *iridescence*.
pearl diver A diver who repeatedly goes underwater to bring up oysters and mussels that may contain gemstone-quality pearls.
pearl oysters A general term, not a specific name, for several kinds of oysters and mussels capable of growing gemstone-quality pearls.
pearl sac Material that surrounds foreign matter introduced into a MOLLUSK and eventually grows into a pearl.
periculture Pearl farming, aimed at creating CULTURED PEARLS on a water farm; sometimes called *aquaculture*.
saltwater pearls Pearls grown inside the bodies of MOLLUSKS that live in bodies of saltwater.
scuba gear Special gear that provides air as needed from tanks worn on a diver's back. The name is short for *self-contained underwater breathing apparatus*.
seeding: See GRAFTING.
seed pearls Pearls so small and light that they look very much like seeds.
synthetic pearls: See IMITATION PEARLS.

On the Internet

The Internet has many interesting sites about pearls The site addresses often change, so the best way to find current addresses is to go to a search site, such as www.yahoo.com. Type in a word or phrase, such as "pearls."

As this book was being written, websites about pearls included:

http://www.amnh.org/exhibitions/pearls/
American Museum of Natural History online accompaniment to their exhibit on pearls, including information on the science, history, and culture of pearls.

http://www.pbs.org/wgbh/nova/pearl/
The Perfect Pearl, a section of the Nova Online website, including how pearls are cultured, dangers to pearls, and history of pearls, plus educational resources and links to related websites.

http://www.com.univ–mrs.fr/IRD/atollpol/resatoll/perlicul/ukperli.htm
Pearl Farming in the Polynesian Atolls, offering descriptions and images of how pearls are cultured in the South Pacific.

http://minerals.usgs.gov/minerals/pubs/commodity/gemstones/sp14–95/pearls.html
Section of the U.S. Geological Survey website describing the history of freshwater pearls and pearl farming in the United States.

In Print

Your local library system will have various books on pearls. The following is just a sampling of them.

Dickinson, Joan Younger. *The Book of Pearls.* New York: Crown, 1968.

Donkin, R. A. *Beyond Price.* Philadelphia: American Philosophical Society, 1998.

Farn, Alexander E. *Pearls.* London: Butterworths, 1990.

Franck, Irene M., and David M. Brownstone. *The Green Encyclopedia.* New York: Prentice Hall, 1992.

Joyce, Kristin, and Shellei Addison. *Pearls.* New York: Simon & Schuster, 1993.

Landman, Neal H., et al. *Pearls: A Natural History.* New York: Harry N. Abrams, 2001.

Matlins, Antoinette L. *The Pearl.* Woodstock, NY: Gemstone Press, 1995.

Taburiaux, Jean. *Pearls.* Radnor, PA: Chilton, 1985.

Van Nostrand's Scientific Encyclopedia, 8th ed., 2 vols. Douglas M. Considine and Glenn D. Considine, eds. New York: Van Nostrand Reinhold, 1995.

Young, Eleanor R. *Pearls.* New York: Franklin Watts, 1970.

Pearls

Index

Africa 14
Americas 14–16
Annam 14
aquaculture 22, 30
aragonite 9, 30
Asia 14, 23, 29
Australia 15, 26, 29
Aztecs 15

Bahrain 13, 15
baroque pearls 7, 9, 30
bends 20–21, 30
bivalves 5, 30
blister pearls 7, 23, 30
Buddhists 12
Burma 15, 29
Byzantines 11

calcium 9, 30
calcium carbonate 9, 30
carbon 9, 30
Caribbean Sea 14–15
Central America 14–15
Central Asia 14
Ceylon 14–15
Chesapeake Bay 26–27
China 12, 14–15, 22–23, 29
color 4, 8, 10
Columbus, Christopher 15
conchiolin 9, 30
crystal 9, 30
cultivating pearls 5, 21–25, 27–30
cultured pearls 5, 8–10, 21–25, 29–30

decompression sickness 20, 30
Diana, Princess 16
Dilmun 13
diving 17–21, 24, 30
diving suits 17–18, 20
dust pearls 9, 30

ears, damage to 19–21
East Africa 14
East Asia 14
Elizabeth, Queen 13
England 13

Europe 13, 15, 23

Far East 23
fertilizers 26–27
foreign matter 6–9, 22–25, 30
France 6
free pearls 8, 30
freshwater 4–6, 14, 16–17, 28–30

gemstones 4–6, 8, 11–14, 16, 30
Germany 12
grafting 25, 28–30
Great Age of Pearls 13
Great Shellfish Bay 26
Guangxi 14
Guangzhou 14
Gulf War 28

Hainan 14–15
Hindus 12
Holy Roman Empire 12

imitation pearls 5, 10, 30
implantation 23–25, 30
India 11–12, 14–15
Indian Ocean 12–13, 16, 20
Indonesia 15, 29
invertebrates 4, 30
Iran 13, 15, 28
Iraq 13, 15, 28
iridescence 4, 7, 30
Italy 9

Japan 15, 19, 23–24, 27
jewelry 6–7, 9–14, 16
Josephine, Empress 6

Kuwait 13, 15

Land of Pearls 15
lining 6–8, 30
luster 4, 7–8, 30

Mannar, Gulf of 14–15, 18
mantle 6–10, 30
Maryland 26

Mayans 15
medicine 12
Meizhou Island 24
Mexico 15, 29
Mexico, Gulf of 28
Middle East 11
Mikimoto, Kochiki 23–25
Mississippi River Valley 8, 14–15, 25
mollusks 4–10, 21, 24, 26, 29–30
Mongolia 14–15
mother-of-pearl 6–8, 23, 30
muscle 7, 30
Muslims 12
mussels 5–6, 14, 17, 21–26, 29–30
Myanmar 15, 29

nacre 6, 8, 23, 25, 30
Napoleon (Bonaparte), Emperor 6
Native Americans 26
natural pearls 5–16, 21–22, 29–30
New World 14–15
Nicaragua 15
nitrogen 19–20, 30
North America 29
nucleation 25, 30
nucleus 6, 9, 23–25, 30

oil 13, 28
Oman 13, 15
orient 4, 7–8, 30
Otto I, Emperor
oysters 5–6, 15, 17, 21, 23–30

Panama 15
Pearl Coast 15–16
pearl fishing 12–21, 28, 30
Pearl of Allah 9
pearl oysters 5, 17, 30
pearl sac 8, 30
perliculture 22, 30
Persian Gulf 13, 15, 17–18, 28

Philippines 15, 29
pigtoe 23, 29
pollution 26–29
Polynesia 15, 29

Qatar 13, 15

Red Sea 14–15, 17
red tide 26
religious use 11–12, 14–15
Romans 11

saltwater 4–6, 13–17, 22, 28–30
sand 6
Saudi Arabia 13–15
scuba gear 20–21, 24, 30
seeding 25, 30
seed pearls 9, 16, 30
shape 6–9
shell 5–10, 22–23, 25, 30
shellfish 4, 27, 30
Siberia 14–15
size 7–9, 11
slaves 21
South America 14
South China Sea 24
Southeast Asia 14, 29
South Pacific 10
Spain 15–16
Sri Lanka 14–15
stringing 10, 25
synthetic pearls 10, 30

Tahiti 10
Theodora, Empress 11
Toltecs 15

United Arab Emirates 13, 15
United States 14–15

Venezuela 15–16
vertebrates 4
Vietnam 14–15
Virginia 26

waste 26–27
water pressure 19–20

Edison Twp. Free Public Library
340 Plainfield Ave.
Edison, New Jersey 08817